The History of Football

Frances Mackay

1891 football match

Photo credits

The publishers would like to thank the following sources for their kind permission to reproduce the pictures used in this book:

Allsport – cover page, pages 3, 7, 10, 11, 12, 19
Hulton Getty – pages 18, 19
Mary Evans Picture Library – pages, 4, 13, 20
POPPERFOTO – page 5
Public Record Office – pages 18, 21

Acknowledgements

We are especially grateful to Sir Bobby Charlton for agreeing to write a short autobiography for this book.

Thanks also to Kevin Massey for help with research.

Page 14 © Times Newspaper Limited, 31st July 1966.

Published by Hopscotch Educational Publishing Ltd,
29 Waterloo Place, Leamington Spa CV32 5LA
Tel: 01926 744227

© 2001 Hopscotch Educational Publishing

Written by Frances Mackay
Series design by Blade Communications
Illustrated by Dave Burroughs
Printed by Clintplan, Southam

Frances Mackay hereby asserts her moral right to be identified as the author of this work in accordance with the Copyright, Designs and Patents Act, 1988.

ISBN 1-902239-90-3

Contents

Chapter 1: The game

Who invented football?

No-one really knows for sure who invented football.

In China, a football report was found that was written 2000 years ago.

The Japanese played a ball game called kenatt during the 14th century.

The Ancient Greeks and Romans also played team games with a ball.

In Britain, it is thought that the first ball games were played using a pig's bladder. Records show that the game was played in the streets of London as early as 1175.

16th Century football

THE HISTORY OF FOOTBALL

What was the early game of football like?

In Britain the first games of football probably started as an annual event near the time of Shrove Tuesday.

Early painting of football, at the time of Edward II

The boys and young men would play the game in the streets of the cities and towns.

It was a very rough and noisy game. There were no rules.

Many players were hurt. Sometimes people died.

Sometimes hundreds of players would join in!

The game could go on all day long.

People who tried to ban early football

Many kings of England tried to stop football from being played.

Edward II (1307-1327)

Edward II banned football because it was too noisy and rough. People caught playing could be sent to prison.

Edward III (1327-1377)

Edward III tried to put an end to football because he felt the men were not spending enough time on archery and javelin throwing.

Richard II (1377-1399) and Henry IV (1399-1413)

also tried to ban football.

Henry VII (1485-1509)

During the reign of Henry VII a proclamation was made that forbade people to play football or golf.

How football became organised

Why did football not die out?

Although many people tried to ban football, the players enjoyed it so much that they played it wherever they could and the game continued.

Who invented the first rules?

Football began to be played by boys at public schools and Universities. It was the public schools that first wrote down the rules of the game. However, each school had its own different set of rules.

1860

When were a common set of rules drawn up?

In 1848 people from the main public schools met together to decide on a common set of rules. These became known as the Cambridge Rules.

Which was the first football club?

Sheffield Club was the first football club, formed in 1857.

The early rules of football

The Uppingham Rules of 1862.

1 A goal is scored whenever the ball is forced through the goal and under the bar, except it be thrown by hand.

2 Hands may be used only to stop a ball and place it on the ground before the feet.

3 Kicks must be aimed only at the ball.

4 A player may not kick the ball whilst in the air.

5 No tripping up or heel kicking allowed.

6 Whenever a ball is kicked beyond the side flags, it must be returned by the player who kicked it, from the spot it passed the flag line, in a straight line towards the middle of the ground.

7 When a ball is kicked behind the line of goal, it shall be kicked off from that line by one of the side whose goal it is.

8 No player may stand within six paces of the kicker when he is kicking off.

9 A player is 'out of play' immediately he is in front of the ball, and must return behind the ball as soon as possible. If the ball is kicked by his own side past a player, he may not touch or kick it, or advance, until one of the other side has first kicked it, or one of his own side has been able to kick it on a level with, or in front of him.

10 No charging allowed when a player is out of play; that is, immediately the ball is behind him.

Referees

Early football games did not have referees.

When teams began to compete for the Football Association Cup in 1872 there was a need for someone to settle any disputes. So each team had an umpire.

The umpires kept an eye on the game but they could not interfere with it.

By 1874 the umpires were allowed to give a free kick for handball and could send players off when they broke the rules.

Sometimes the two umpires could not agree so it was decided to appoint someone not linked to either team. This person was the referee.

In the 1891/92 season, referees were given the powers they have today. The two umpires became linesmen or assistant referees.

Did You Know?

It was the Oxford University students of the 1880s who invented the name 'soccer'. The word is an abbreviation of 'association'.

The players

**Since football began, there have been many players
who have developed into excellent footballers.
Here are two of the more famous ones.**

Sir Stanley Matthews

Many people think that Stanley Matthews was the first great footballer of modern times.

He was born in Stoke-on-Trent in 1915.

He turned professional in 1932 with Stoke City.

In 1934 he played for England against Wales.

In 1946 he was sold to Blackpool for £11,500 but returned to Stoke City in 1961.

Matthews played a total of 54 games for England.

His nickname was the 'Wizard of Dribble'.

During the 1930s and 1940s Matthews was considered to be the best outside-right in the world.

He was very popular with the fans.

He retired in 1965 at the age of 50, making him the oldest player ever to play First Division football. He was also knighted in 1965.

Sir Stanley Matthews

Football time line

Football Association formed	FA Cup began	First international game played – England v Scotland	Scottish FA Cup began
1863	**1871**	**1872**	**1873**

Sir Bobby Charlton

I was born in Ashington, England, on October 11th, 1937. I never found the game difficult, even at a young age and I could control and pass a ball well because I came from a football family. My uncle, Jackie Milburn, played for Newcastle United and my brother, Jack, was also a famous player.

1961

I signed as a junior for Manchester United when I was 15 and I made my debut at 18 when we played against Charlton Athletic.

Everyone dreams of playing in an FA Cup final because of the prestige of playing at Wembley, the glamour of the occasion and the fact that the Queen was there. It's something every footballer dreams of, so I was very proud to play in my first final at 19.

I played for England in the World Cups of 1962, 1966 and 1970. I think winning the World Cup in 1966 was one of our country's greatest sporting moments.

I retired from Manchester United in 1973 and even though I've stopped playing, lots of people still want to talk to me about football. Football has been marvellous for me. I've had a great life. I think that if you work hard, concentrate and try to improve in whatever it is you want to do, then I think you will succeed in any walk of life.

My best wishes
Bobby Charlton

England, Wales, Scotland & Ireland form the International Football Association Board	FA allow professional players	Football League formed	Scottish Football League formed
1882	**1885**	**1888**	**1890**

Black players

It is thought that the world's first black professional league player was Arthur Wharton who began playing in 1889. Between 1919 and 1939 only a small number of black players joined the game, among them Jack Leslie who played for Plymouth Argyle and John Parris who became the first black player to represent a national side (Wales).

During the late 1940s, more Africans and Asians came to live in Britain. This meant that more black players were joining football teams. One well-known player during this time was Jamaican-born Lloyd Lindberg ('Lindy') Delapenha. He played for Middlesbrough between 1950–57.

Jack Leslie 1922

Perhaps the most famous black player during the 1960s was Albert Johanneson who came from South Africa. He played for Leeds and became the first black player to play in an FA Cup final. During the 1970s, Viv Anderson, who played for Nottingham Forest, became the first black player to win a full English cap.

In the late 1980s and 1990s there was a big increase in the number of black players. Before then many players had suffered racial discrimination. In 1991 the government actually made it illegal to chant racist comments at football matches. The numbers of black players continues to rise.

Johanneson 1968

Football time line

The Football League created a Second Division	FIFA was formed	Argentina and Uruguay played the first South American international match	The League formed the Third Division
1892	1904	1906	1920

Women's football

Although some people think that football should only be played by men, women began playing at the same time as men. During the 1890s there was a big increase of interest in the game mainly due to the influence of Nettie Honeywell in England and Lady Florence Dixie in Scotland.

Early women's football

During the First World War, men's and women's teams played against each other to raise money for charities. But in 1921 the FA banned women from playing on Football League grounds. Some people say that this was because the women's games were beginning to draw big crowds and the men did not like this. The ban caused interest to decline and it was not until 1966, when England won the World Cup, that the women's game began to pick up again.

More and more women began to play football and the Women's Football Association (WFA) was founded in 1969. In 1972 the FA dropped their ban on women playing at League grounds. By the late 1980s there were 21 Leagues and over 8000 players. In 1991 the first Women's National League was formed and the FA lifted their ban on mixed football teams for under 11s in schools.

The first England womens' team was formed in 1972 when it won against Scotland 3–2. A European Championship was started in 1982 and the first final of the Women's UEFA Cup was played in 1984. The Women's World Cup began in 1991 and was won by the USA.

The FA Cup left England for the first time to Cardiff	The first World Cup won by Uruguay	Italy won the World Cup	First football match shown on television
1927	**1930**	**1934**	**1936**

Football in the news

extracts from **The Sunday Times,** London. July 31st, 1966

Triumph...

London goes mad after World Cup victory

By Sunday Times Reporters

LONDON went mad last night after England's 4-2 victory in one of the most fantastic finals in the history of the World Cup. The celebrations culminated in a jubilant demonstration in Latin American style outside the hotel in Kensington High Street where a reception was being held for the players.

As the British Government entertained 480 guests from the football world in the new Royal Garden Hotel, the fans yelled the "England, England" chant which has echoed round Wembley in the last three weeks and rose to an incredible crescendo yesterday afternoon.

Cars jammed all the way along the street took up the "England, England" beat on their horns...

...Hundreds more England supporters danced and sang in Trafalgar Square, blowing bugles, ringing bells and sounding horns. The supporters, led by a youth holding up a replica of the World Cup, pranced through the crowds singing "We've got the whole world in our hands."...

...And what a game to remember. In the cauldron of emotion that was Wembley even an hour before kick-off it was like a madhouse. Supporters were just standing cheering as if it was all over and England had already won. During the match people were throwing streamers, screaming at the referee and crying with each England goal...

...Then her Majesty presented the gold cup to Bobby Moore who looked very English and very dignified as he held the Cup aloft ... Bobby Charlton was weeping with emotion as he received his winner's medal from the Queen.

Football time line

Italy won the World Cup	Scottish League Cup created	League attendances reach 40 million for the first time	Uruguay won the World Cup
1938	1946	1948	1950

and tribulation...

extracts from The Times, London. *April 16th, 1989*

Father tells how he fought in vain to save his daughters

A grieving father last night told how he fought in vain to save his two teenage daughters trapped at Hillsborough stadium in Sheffield.

Mr Trevor Hicks, aged 43, helped to give mouth-to-mouth resuscitation to his daughters Sarah, aged 19, and Victoria, aged 15.

But both girls, regular Liverpool supporters who stood on the famous Kop at Anfield, died.

Mr Hicks, managing director of a West Midlands company, said: "Football was the one thing we did as a family and now we are not a family any more."

His wife Jenny, aged 42, was also at the match but had a seat in one of the stands...

..."The girls and I got into the ground around 2 pm. They were in a different section to me. They were there in good time which meant they were down the front and that was the problem", Mr Hicks said.

"I could see that where the girls were was getting very crowded.

"I shouted to one of the senior officers that people were being crushed...

"I saw Victoria being passed over the heads of people and over the fence and on to the pitch. I managed to get on to the pitch and there were Sarah and Victoria lying there...

..."I think the fence was partly to blame. It was too strong."

"Also, I think the police were so busy trying to prevent a pitch invasion that they didn't see what was happening."

...The death toll in the Hillsborough football tragedy had risen to 94 last night...The youngest was a boy of 10 and the oldest a man aged 62...

UEFA formed. West Germany won the World cup	Brazil won the World Cup	Brazil won the World cup	Tottenham became the first British Club to win a European trophy
1954	**1958**	**1962**	**1963**

Chapter 2: Equipment

The pitch

When football was first played there was no pitch at all. The game was often played in the streets of towns and cities and no boundaries were necessary.

However, once clubs started to have their own grounds in the late 1800s, they decided to mark out the boundaries of the pitch. Kick-offs required that the centre of the ground was also marked. A circle 10 yards (9.15m) in radius was drawn around the centre spot because there was a rule that said players had to be 10 yards away from a kick-off.

In 1891 penalties were introduced, so two lines were marked across the field at 12 and 18 yards from each goal line.

These markings lasted until 1902 when the markings used today were introduced (see the diagram on the facing page).

1891

1902

Football time line

Stanley Matthews (50) became the oldest man to play a First Division match	England won the World Cup	Celtic won the European Cup	Manchester United was the first English side to win the European Cup
1965	**1966**	**1967**	**1968**

The International Board has approved the following table of metric equivalents for the Laws of the Game.

130yd	= 120.00m
100yd	= 90.00m
50yd	= 45.00m
12yd	= 11.00m
10yd	= 9.15m
8yd	= 7.32m
6yd	= 5.50m
1yd	= 1.00m
(actually	= 0.9144m)

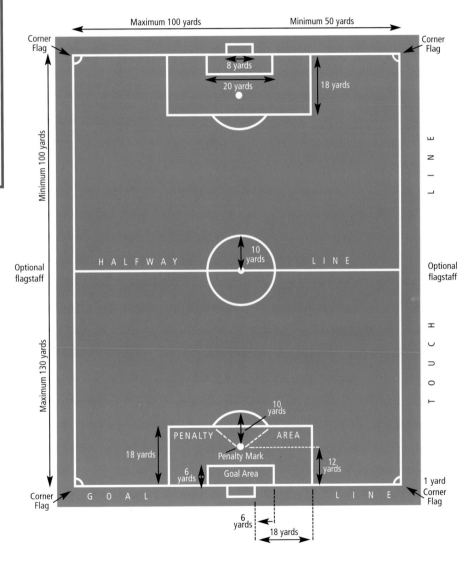

Brazil won the World Cup	Liverpool was the first to win the League Title and European Trophy in the same season	West Germany won the World Cup.	Argentina won the World Cup
1970	**1973**	**1974**	**1978**

Footballs

The first footballs were pig's bladders, blown up and knotted at the end like a balloon. Later, a leather case was made to go around the pig's bladder. The ball was therefore plum shaped because it matched the shape of the bladder.

In 1862 the rubber bladder was invented and a pump was used to inflate it. The ball became more rounded although many balls still had a button at each end to hold the panels of leather together. 'Buttonless' footballs began to be made in the 1880s.

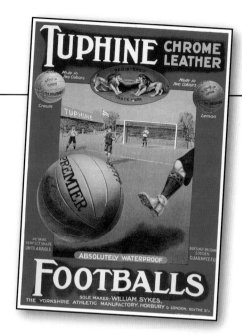

1909

Before 1866 footballs could be any size but after this date it was agreed that the circumference be no more than 28 inches (71cm) and no less than 27 inches (68cm). In 1889 a standard weight was introduced (12–15 ounces) but this was changed to 14–16 ounces (396g–453g) in 1937.

Early footballs were not waterproof so they became very heavy when used in wet weather. This made it very dangerous for players to head the ball. Today's footballs are waterproof.

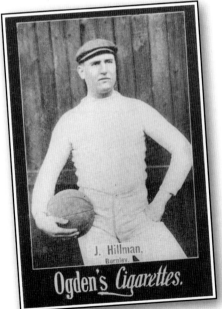

Jack Hillman

Football time line

Italy won the World Cup	Argentina won the World Cup	West Germany won the World Cup	The end of artificial pitches in Division One
1982	**1986**	**1990**	**1991**

Footballs

1922
A man using a machine to lace-up a football

1923
Inflating a football with a pump

How modern footballs are made

1 The outer material (usually vulcanised rubber, polyurethane, PVC or leather) is stuck to the linings using natural rubber latex.
2 It is then dried and cured to make a flexible sheet of football material.
3 The material is cut into 18 or 26 panels with pre-punched stitching holes.
4 The panels are cleaned.
5 The panels are printed using special inks.
6 The panels are sorted, weighed and matched to the correct bladder weight.
7 The panels and bladder set is then sent to be hand stitched. This takes about three hours. The ball is first stitched inside out then it is turned the right way round and the final panel is stitched.
8 The ball is inflated and checked for any faults.
9 The ball is cleaned and packed ready for sale.

1936
Lady holding footballs made at a factory in Southwark

1966
World Cup football

The English First Division broke away from the Football League to form the Premiership	Brazil won the World Cup	Manchester United were the first English team to win successive doubles	France won the World Cup
1992	**1994**	**1996**	**1998**

Shirts and shorts

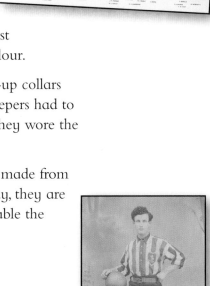
1881

Shirts

The first football shirts were often made from thick wool. They tended to stretch out of shape, became very heavy in the rain and could be itchy! These early shirts had a lace-up collar. Teams did not necessarily have different coloured shirts. They were identified by the different colours of their caps or socks. Some teams wore coloured armbands. But by the time of the first FA Cup Final in 1872, most teams had chosen a team colour.

By 1911 most shirts were made from cotton and the lace-up collars were replaced by buttons. It wasn't until 1913 that goalkeepers had to wear different colours. Until then they wore the same shirt as their team-mates.

From the 1960s shirts began to be made from synthetics rather than cotton. Today, they are made from special fabrics that enable the player to keep cool.

1900

Shorts

The first footballers played in full-length trousers but as the game developed and players wanted to be able to move more freely, they wore shorter knickerbockers cut just above the knee. The shorts became shorter after World War II. Shorts were very baggy in the 1930s (and again in the 1990s) but were much tighter in the 1970s.

1932

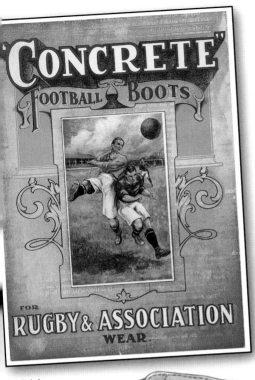

1911

Boots

early 1800s

Early players did not have special boots for football. They simply wore their everyday boots.

1930s

Studs were nailed into working boots for matches.

1950s

The black with white trim (still used today) began to be used in the 1950s. The boot came below the ankle so there was less protection but the players had more freedom of movement.

1990s

Top quality boots in the 1990s were made from kangaroo leather with plastic soles and aluminium studs.

Glossary

advance
to go or bring forward

annual
to happen every year

artificial
made by people, not found naturally

ban
to stop something

bladder
a sac in the body that holds urine

a hollow bag that becomes round
when filled with air

boundaries
the marked limits of a playing area

circumference
the distance around a circle

compete
to take part in a contest or competition

cured
preserved leather

debut
the first time a player has played
in public

dispute
to argue or quarrel

founded
when an organisation is first set up

goal
a score

handball
when a player touches the ball
with a hand

illegal
against the law

inflate
to fill up with air

international
involving two or more countries

kenatt
a ball game played in Japan in the 1300s

kick-off
the first kick from the centre spot that
begins a game or restarts a game
after a goal

latex
a milky fluid made by some plants and
used to make rubber

league
an association of sporting clubs

linesmen
assistants to the referee

national
of a nation as a whole

penalties
punishment against players for illegal play or a shoot-out to determine a winner when the score is even

pitch
the field of play

polyurethane
a synthetic material

prestige
high status, very important

proclamation
public announcement

professional
earning money for playing

public school
private fee-paying school

PVC
polyvinyl chloride

racial discrimination
showing dislike for people of a different race

radius
the distance from the centre of a circle to the circumference

referee
the official person who controls discipline, keeps time and makes decisions about rules during a match

Shrove Tuesday
the last day before Lent begins at Easter

stadium
a sports arena with seats

studs
round objects on the bottom of football boots to give better grip

synthetic
artificial

tribulation
great unhappiness

triumph
great happiness resulting from victory

vulcanised rubber
rubber treated to make it stronger and more elastic

waterproof
will not let water in

Index